Jump Start Your Career
in Technology & IT
in about 100 Pages

Table of Contents

Let's Start !

Chapter 1 Conceptual Overview

MVC is Microsoft's latest offering for designing and building web applications, and it is also an architectural design pattern. As a design pattern, MVC and its variant patterns have been around for some time but the framework is still relatively new, giving it the advantage of having learned from earlier frameworks. If you are familiar with other web development frameworks, then you can trace the history of key features and see how common problems are avoided. However, this book is not intended to be a history lesson. For the present, be aware that MVC incorporates lessons learned from many systems and is not in itself "a thing".

The Design Pattern

To better understand the framework, we need to understand the design pattern on which it is based. MVC and its variant patterns (MVP, Passive View, etc.) separate a web app into three distinct areas: the model, the view, and the controller. The model is the data that the app uses, the view is the user interface (UI), and the controller houses most of the app's logic which ties the three pieces together.

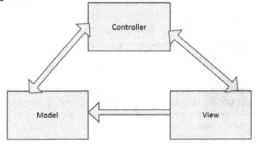

Figure 1: Components in the MVC pattern

To effectively use MVC, adhere to the following best practices:

- The model should be a simple object with read and write properties to support a single view.
- The view should focus on standards-based markup.
- Logic in the view should be limited to user interaction and not include business logic.
- Controllers should not know anything about how the data in the model is manipulated in the view.
- Controllers should not know anything about how the data is persisted beyond the model.

Following these guiding principles will help ensure that we stay out of trouble.

> The difference between the MVC, MVP, Passive View, and other design patterns is a matter of how much responsibility you give the various components. These are subtle differences that we can safely ignore for now.

A Brief Discussion on Web Forms

If you are already familiar with developing web apps with Web Forms, MVC will be a paradigm shift for you. To fully appreciate the power and appeal of the framework, let's review some of the limitations of Web Forms and point out some of the advantages of MVC.

Many of these limitations become less relevant with each new release of Web Forms and can be mitigated further with best practices. But the following remain the common problems plaguing many Web Forms apps:

- View state
- Bloated HTML
- Page life cycle
- Awkward URLs
- Testability

 Note: You will find it much easier to integrate client-side functionality to a controller than to a Web Form's code-behind. Actions in controllers make natural endpoints for AJAX calls. We can easily build up the URL for the endpoint. We do not have to struggle to identify and track the IDs of HTML components. View models, along with the model binder (which we will soon explore), make it easy to translate data back and forth.

MVC builds on the stateless nature of the web. In many Web Forms apps, app state is maintained in server-side code with view state required to remind the server of everything that has happened so far. Getting rid of view state eliminates a lot of what is passed back and forth between the server and browser. This alone makes pages load faster.

While view state accounts for most of the bloat in the markup, we are able reduce it further with a stronger focus on standards-compliant markup. With Web Forms' focus on server controls, developers often had little control over the markup that was ultimately sent to the browser. The situation has improved with each release of the framework, but developers still relinquish substantial control of the generated markup. With MVC, developers still may not have complete control, but the functionality they are now provided is more focused on producing clean, standards-compliant markup. With Web Forms, the developer has a large volume of work to perform to get clean markup. With MVC, the developer has to work hard to avoid producing clean markup—a transition that turns the workflow on its head.

 Note: Standards-compliant markup makes it easier to integrate with client-side libraries such as jQuery, Knockout, and AngularJS.

The page life cycle has been abandoned altogether in MVC. Each request is truly stateless. State is more easily maintained in the page than on the server. Each page request has an associated action; the logic executed during the request can be traced from this one method. This simplifies troubleshooting and maintenance. You do not have to follow through the events of the page life cycle to track down what logic is being run.

For many, the most important innovation is the improved testability. It is difficult to build automated unit tests against a Web Form, but it is relatively straightforward to build test cases against the logic in the controller. A Web Form is riddled with complex UI elements such as text boxes, as well as **Session**, **HTTPContext**, and much more. In MVC, controllers deal with view models and similar objects that can be mocked with relative ease to simplify testing.

 Tip: You cannot access the Document Object Model (DOM) from the controller, but you could access anything else exposed in the Request object. Don't be tempted. Let the framework handle manipulating query strings, forms collections, etc. You should focus only on manipulating the model.

More Than Just a Pattern

The MVC framework is more than just a pattern. MVC apps implement the MVC design pattern because Microsoft has brought more to the table than simply helping developers maintain good practices. The framework does a lot of the heavy lifting for us, making it easier to follow good coding standards and build robust web apps.

Throughout this book, we will explore:

- View engines
- Model binders
- Display and editor templates
- HTML helpers
- Filters

View engines make it easier to produce the HTML we need. Razor, the default view engine in ASP.NET MVC, has a streamlined syntax injection model that allows developers to use a template-driven approach, which makes it easier to create a consistent look and feel for your site. Model binders handle taking data the user entered in the view and repopulating the model. Not only do they handle automatically pulling data in from the view, they will also run any validations associated with the model, which will free you up to work on more pressing matters such as business logic. We will explore all things validation-related in Chapter 4.

Editor templates take the separation of concerns a step further. As we will soon see, editor templates allow us to simply state that we want an editor for a particular property without getting bogged down specifying the form that the editor should take.

HTML helpers are a great compromise between a drag-and-drop designer approach and the tedium of writing all of the HTML by hand. Anyone who has trusted a drag-and-drop approach to get everything right has been burned, but having to write all of the markup by hand is tedious and potentially error-prone. With HTML helpers, we get simple methods that we can call to handle much of the heavy lifting, without sacrificing any of the control. We can also easily write our own helpers to cover any scenarios missed by the built-in helpers.

Filters are attributes that we can add to actions or the controller as a whole. Filters have logic associated with them. All we need to do to get this logic or new behavior is to add the appropriate filter to an action.

Don't worry, you can build effective MVC apps long before you understand these concepts. But, as you learn more about these concepts, you will discover how the framework can do more of our work for us.

Summary

MVC is both a design pattern and a framework for building web apps following this pattern. The framework builds on what has worked well with other frameworks and manages to avoid some common pitfalls that have plagued others.

Chapter 2 MVC Says Hello World

When you create a new MVC web app in Visual Studio, you will have a functional web app out of the box. Visual Studio will create the directory structure that the framework expects and will provide default content for key files based on templates that we will explore in Chapter 6. This will not be a useful app, but it does have all of the pieces in place to run. Let's get started.

The screenshots in this book are taken from Visual Studio 2013. I am also using the 2012-compatible templates because I believe this gives you a better breakdown of your template options. Other versions of Visual Studio may look a bit different.

Our First Application

In Visual Studio, create a new ASP.NET MVC 4 Web Application and give it a meaningful name.

Figure 2: Creating the initial app

You will then be prompted for a few other details about this new app.

We will be using the Razor view engine, so keep that option selected. We will more thoroughly discuss view engines later.

Choosing a template is a bit tougher and depends on what you are trying to do. In most cases, your choice will boil down to deciding between an Internet app and an intranet app.

If you select an empty template, you can still easily build an Internet, intranet, mobile, or any other type of app. Adding a web API is easy, as is building a single-page app. The only difference is how much work is already done for you and how that work was done. For this book, we will use the **Internet Application** template. This means that it will include an `AccountController` and supporting views to handle authentication as well as password resets and changes. If you start with an intranet app, the resulting app will not include the `AccountController` but would, instead, rely on Windows authentication to handle authentication and authorization.

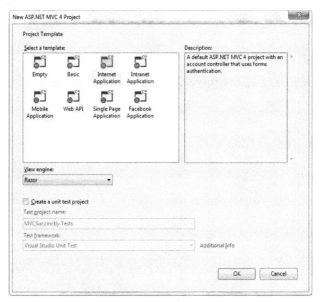

Figure 3: Selecting the Internet Application template

The templates provided are just that: they give you a starting point to build on.

 Note: Because testability is a big deal in MVC, you are prompted to create a unit test project as well. If you set this up, you can use a unit testing tool to test all of the business logic in your controller. This is a good practice to follow but outside the scope of this book.

Once Visual Studio is finished creating our initial project, it will look similar to the following screenshot.

Figure 4: Solution Explorer for new MVC project

At this point, we have a functional MVC web app. Press F5 to run it. You should see something similar to the following in your web browser.

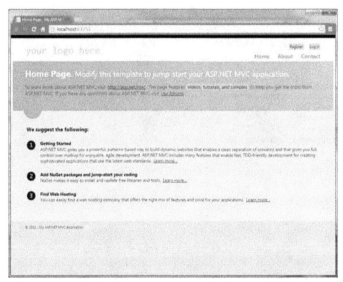

Figure 5: Our simple app in action

Note: Depending on the version of Visual Studio and the framework used, the appearance of your initial app may differ from what is shown in Figure 5. This is because of differences in the layout and the style sheets for the selected templates that shipped with your version of Visual Studio.

Congratulations! You have your first running MVC app. Now let's make it do something interesting.

Introducing Models

Let's work on making this app useful. To start, we will define a model to hold data that we want to display. In the **Solution Explorer**, right-click **Models**, and then select **Class**. Our model will start off rather simple.

```
public class GreetingModel
{
    public string Name { get; set; }
    public string Greeting { get; set; }
}
```

Code Listing 1: Initial view model

Once we create a model, we can change the `Index` action of the `HomeController` to use it. The `HomeController` was automatically created in the controllers folder based on the template we started with. Once you make the changes, your action should look like the following code listing.

```
using System;
using System.Collections.Generic;
using System.Linq;
using System.Web;
using System.Web.Mvc;
using MVCSuccinctly.Models;

namespace MVCSuccinctly.Controllers
{
    public class HomeController : Controller
    {
        public ActionResult Index()
        {
            var model = new GreetingModel
            {
                Greeting = "Welcome to the World of MVC",
                Name = "Your friendly neighborhood MVC App"
            };
            return View(model);
```

```
        }
      }
   }
```

Code Listing 2: Initial action

 Note: Don't forget to add a *using* **statement at the top to refer to the**
MVCSuccinctly.Models **namespace where we put our model. All other** *using* **statements**
are automatically added by the template.

In addition to creating the controller that we just looked at, the template will create initial
versions of the supporting views needed for this controller. We now need to change the view to
use the model passed in from the controller. We can easily navigate to this view by right-clicking
inside the body of the action and selecting **Go to View** from the context menu. We start by
associating the model to the view. We add the following code as the first line in our view, which
will be in the **Home** folder under **Views** and will have the same name as our action.

```
@model MVCSuccinctly.Models.GreetingModel
```

Code Listing 3: Specify the data type for the model

 Tip: You can also select Add View from the context menu and Visual Studio will add a
new view in the Views folder for this controller, so you do not need to worry about
getting the files in the right place.

Now, when we refer to **Model** in our view, it will have the values that we specified in the action.
We add the following code to our view.

```
<hgroup class="title">
    <h2>@Model.Greeting</h2>
    <h3>@Model.Name</h3>

</hgroup>
```

Code Listing 4: Initial view

Note: *@Model is a property of the view that refers to the model that was passed to the view from the controller. This property is strongly typed based on the data type specified in the @model directive at the top of the view.*

@model and @Model look similiar but they are very different. @model occurs only once and specifies the data type of the model. @Model allows you to reference the value for the model passed to the view.

If everything has worked as expected, pressing F5 to run the app should give us the following, with our new content highlighted in the black box which I added with some simple cascading style sheets (CSS) to highlight the difference.

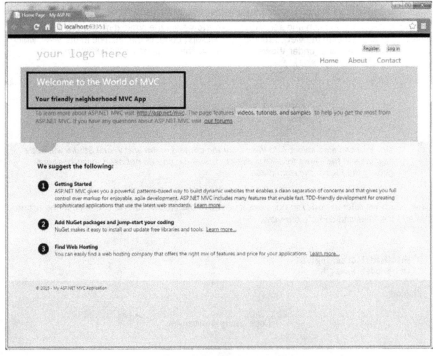

Figure 6: Our initial app

Our view is written using the Razor view engine. The view engine is responsible for much of the magic of writing simple HTML. Out of the box, MVC ships with two view engines, Razor and ASPX. The ASPX view engine was specifically designed to ease the transition from Web Forms or classic ASP. It uses the familiar <% %> syntax. Razor was designed to be a more streamlined syntax, taking into account lessons learned from various generations and variations of merging code with markup. Razor understands C# code as well as VB.NET, depending on the language selected when you created the app. Because it understands both languages, it can figure out on its own when a code block has ended. There is no need to terminate the code block. Plus, Razor uses a single character "@" to start a code block rather than the traditional two-character <% and %>, which most web developers are familiar with.

Value Substitution

We have already seen an example of this when we substituted the value of a property in our model. Value substitution is simply injecting the value of a variable, property, or method call into the markup. You will probably do this often. While value substitution is limited to a single expression, this still gives you a great deal of flexibility.

You can call a method:

```
<span>@DateTime.Now.ToLongDateString()</span>
```

You can access properties:

```
<h3>@Model.Name</h3>
```

You can access local variables:

```
<li class="@style">
```

Code Blocks

While simple value substitutions are limited to a single expression, code blocks are literally blocks of code. You can declare variables, evaluate if statements, iterate through loops, define your own functions, and more.

A code block will look like this:

```
@{
    if (!string.IsNullOrEmpty(Model.Greeting))
    {
        <span>@Model.Greeting</span>
    }
}
```

Code Listing 5: A basic code block

Or like this:

```
@{
    var style = "morningTheme";
    if (DateTime.Now.Hour > 12)
    {
        style = "eveningTheme";
    }
}
```

Code Listing 6: Another basic code block

 Note: Refer to ASP.NET MVC 4 Mobile Websites Succinctly **for an example of why you might want to have alternate views. Any logic that you place in the view cannot be easily tested and testability is a big deal in MVC. Also, this logic would need to be duplicated if you have alternate views.**

Even though we can put logic in the view, we need to limit it. A good rule of thumb is to limit logic in code blocks to logic that is related to the view. For example, you could use an **if** statement to determine the CSS class to use or a loop to iterate through the items in a list, or you could convert a list to a **List<SelectListItem>**, etc.

Later chapters will show that even this logic can often be avoided, further reducing the amount of logic housed in the view.

HTML Helpers

HTML helpers make it easier to create the markup and produce clean markup. Using them makes it easier to write your markup and also ensures that the generated markup is properly structured and well-formatted.

These helpers are defined as extension methods to the **HTMLHelper** class, and using one is as easy as calling a method.

```
@Html.LabelFor(m => m.UserName)
@Html.TextBoxFor(m => m.UserName)
```

Code Listing 7: Calling an HTML helper

Here we create a label and input a text box for one property from the model passed to the view. The **LabelFor** helper will create an HTML label tag with the property name. If the property includes a **DisplayAttribute**, its value will be displayed. Otherwise, the name of the property will be displayed.

The **TextBoxFor** helper creates an input text box by using the property names to generate the **id** and its value for the initial value of the text box.

There are a lot of helpers available for creating any type of input that you need:

- **ActionLink**
- **BeginForm**
- **CheckBoxFor**
- **DropDownListFor**
- **EditorFor**
- **HiddenFor**
- **PasswordFor**
- **RadioButtonFor**
- **TextAreaFor**
- **ValidationMessageFor**

 Tip: Whenever possible, you should use an HTML helper to generate your markup. An HTML helper will reduce the amount of markup you have to create, ensure that it is standards-complaint, and ensure that your markup works well with the rest of the framework.

Layouts

You may have noticed that in all of our markup so far, we haven't included any details for adding style sheets or JavaScript files, yet each view still looks similar to the others. It may not be immediately obvious where this formatting comes from. If you are used to web development in an ASP.NET environment, you may be looking for the master page, and you would still be using master pages if you were using the ASP.NET view engine. Because we are using the Razor view engine, we are interested in the **Layout** file. This file is located in **\Views\Shared_Layout.cshtml** or **_Layout.vbhtml**.

Let's look at some of the basics for this file. In its simplest form, it may look like the following code listing.

```
<!DOCTYPE html>
<html>
    <head>
        <meta charset="utf-8"/>
        <meta name="viewport"content="width=device-width"/>
        <title>@ViewBag.Title</title>
        @Styles.Render("~/Content/css")
        @Scripts.Render("~/bundles/modernizr")
    </head>
    <body>
        @RenderBody()
        @Scripts.Render("~/bundles/jquery")
```

```
    @RenderSection("scripts", required: false)
  </body>
</html>
```

Code Listing 8: A basic layout

The key area of interest for us at this point is the **@RenderBody** statement. This line of code will render any markup that we have in our views at this location. So, this puts our views in a larger context to the rest of the app.

The calls to `Styles.Render` and `Scripts.Render` are also rather important. MVC allows us to easily bundle scripts and style sheets to make the page load faster. One large style sheet downloads faster than multiple small style sheets because of the overhead of making multiple HTTP calls to get the data. This is a key optimization option that is easy to implement and can have a substantial impact depending on the number of style sheets or JavaScript files you are using.

 Note: If you start your project with the Empty or Basic template, you may be missing the bundling components. To resolve this, copy the BundleConfig file from the App_Start folder for another project and then add a call to it in your `Application_Start` **event handler in the** Global.asax:

```
BundleConfig.RegisterBundles(BundleTable.Bundles);
```

Sections

Finally, let's turn our attention to the **RenderSection** method call. Here we define a section, calling it **scripts**, and we mark that it is not required. This tells the framework to look in the view for a section named **scripts**. If one is found, it will be rendered where the **RenderSection** is called regardless of where it shows up in the actual view.

So, how does this look in the view? We will see this a bit later, but the following sample provides a sneak peek.

```
@section scripts
{
<script>

    // JavaScript code here

</script>
}
```

Code Listing 9: Rendering the scripts section

Sections can be used to add any additional content wanted—from style sheets to inline resources—anywhere in the page, with great flexibility. Sections are not limited to adding style sheets and JavaScript files. They can also be used to specify a different location for markup as well. For example, we might define a section for a navigation bar, side bar, or footer. This would allow the layout to control the look, feel, and structure of the page but still allow individual views to have control over the actual content for these areas.

Summary

In this chapter, we have seen that while there are multiple templates available for creating a new MVC app, we will generally want to create either an Internet app or an intranet app depending on how we will handle security. We have also seen how to pass data from the controller to the view by using models.

As we made our first changes to the view, we got our first taste of the Razor view engine, with simple variable substitution and code blocks. We have seen how Razor handles templates for the website through layouts. We have also seen how sections can be added to the layout to allow individual views to add content in specific places in the layout as needed.

Coming up, we will further explore the view engine, and see how the framework and the Razor view engine, specifically, can do more of the work for us in creating a modern, professional-looking MVC web app.

Chapter 3 The World Says Hello Back

A web app involves a two-way conversation with the user. The web app will ask questions in the form of input controls and the user will respond by clicking buttons or links. Sometimes the user may ask a question by clicking a link or selecting a drop-down value and MVC will respond with a new view or a similar `ActionResult`.

To facilitate this conversation, we will need a new model.

```
public class ItineraryItem
{
    public DateTime? When { get; set; }
    public string Description { get; set; }
    public int? Duration { get; set; }
}
```

Code Listing 10: Our first model

We will build on this model, adding additional features throughout the rest of this chapter.

Adding a Controller

Now that we have this model, let's add a new `ItineraryController`. Let's start with an empty controller. In the **Solution Explorer**, right-click the **Controller** folder, and then select **Add** > **Controller**.

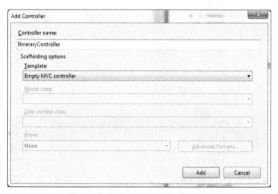

Figure 7: Add a new controller

In the `Create` action, we will allow the user to create a new `ItineraryItem`. Our `Create` action will be simple. See Code Listing 11.

Note: There are other options by selecting different values in the template drop-down menu; you can let the framework automatically fill in more of the pieces for you. We will explore these options later but, for now, we will use an empty controller.

Because we are creating a new `ItineraryItem`, we do not need to initialize it or worry about data mapping.

```
using MVCSuccinctly.Models;
namespace MVCSuccinctly.Controllers
{
    public class ItineraryController : Controller
    {
        public ActionResult Create()
        {
            var model = new ItineraryItem();
            return View(model);
        }
    }
}
```

Code Listing 11: The Create action

Adding the View

Right-click anywhere in the action definition in the code editor. In the context menu, select **Add View**. This will open the **Add View** window.

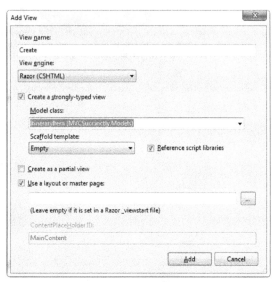

Figure 8: Add View window

We want to create a strongly typed view, and we will specify the model that we just created by selecting it from the **Model class** drop-down. For now, ignore the Scaffold template field; we will explore the options that it provides later. Here, we will stick with an empty template.

We will work through a few iterations of the view, showcasing different features and allowing the framework to do more of the work for us.

In its simplest form, our view should look like the following code listing.

```
@model MVCSuccinctly.Models.ItineraryItem
<h2>Create</h2>
<div class="editor">
@using (Html.BeginForm())
{
    <p>
        @Html.LabelFor(m => m.Description)
        @Html.TextBoxFor(m => m.Description)
        @Html.ValidationMessageFor(m => m.Description)
    </p>
    <p>
        @Html.LabelFor(m => m.When)
        @Html.TextBoxFor(m => m.When)
        @Html.ValidationMessageFor(m => m.When)
    </p>
    <p>
        @Html.LabelFor(m => m.Duration)
```

```
        @Html.TextBoxFor(m => m.Duration)
        @Html.ValidationMessageFor(m => m.Duration)
    </p>
    <p><input  type="submit" value="Save"/></p>
}
</div>
```

Code Listing 12: Simple editor for itinerary items

With this markup, our view will look like the following when we run the app.

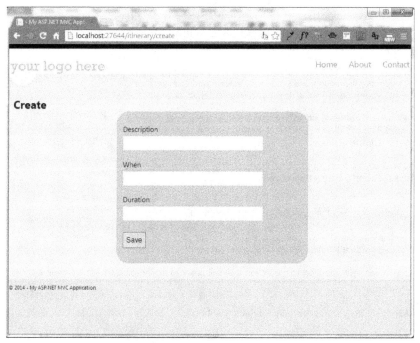

Figure 9: Our first input form

You will notice a few new things in the code sample. The **using** statement is the same **using** statement that you are familiar with from C#. This will wrap the markup in the code block in the form element created by the **BeginForm** HTML helper. With no parameters, the resulting form element will post back. This is the most common usage; however, there are overloads to allow you to specify the controller, the action, POST versus GET methods, as well as specify HTML attributes to be added to the form tag.

Model Binding

`LabelFor`, `TextBoxFor`, and `ValidationMessageFor` are also new and their syntax may seem a bit strange at first. These helper methods use lambda expressions to specify which property to use from the model. Once you become familiar with this syntax, you will discover that it does a great deal for us. By using helpers and extension lambda expressions, we get great IntelliSense that shows us what functionality is and is not available. Many refactoring tools will also catch when a property is renamed and automatically clean up the markup—something that would not be possible if we simply specified the property as an inline string.

By using the `TextBoxFor` HTML helper, we will get markup with the necessary IDs to make it easy to put the values back into the model. Yes, you read that correctly. As long as the view is properly structured, the framework will put the data from the input controls back into your model. This is key to making model binding work.

`LabelFor` will generate an appropriate label for the property specified. We will soon see that this does a bit more than simply output the property name.

`TextBoxFor` will output a text box, starting off with the current value for the specified property and allow the user to edit the value as needed.

`ValidationMessageFor` will output the markup to display any validation messages associated with the specified property. Don't worry about validation messages for now. We will cover them in detail later. For now, the only responsibility the view has is to provide a location for displaying the message.

> Lambda expressions are a succinct way to express an anonymous function. The lambda operator => can be read as "goes to". So the expression
>
> `m => m.When`
>
> can be read as "m goes to m dot When".
>
> m, the value to the left of the lambda operator, is the parameter passed to the function. In this case it will be the model passed to the view.
>
> So m=>m.When is specifying which property of the model to act on.

Let's now turn our attention to the action that will process the response from the user.

```
[HttpPost]
public ActionResult Create(ItineraryItem data)
{
    return View();
}
```

Code Listing 13: Method signature for a basic Create action

We do not care what you do with the data the user entered; you can save it in a database, an XML file, or just persist it in memory. The focus here is on using MVC to interact with the user; however, this simple action will get a bit more complicated before we are done.

Filters

The **HttpPost** attribute in <u>Code Listing 13</u> is an example of a filter. This attribute instructs the framework that this action be called only as a POST and not as a GET. This is necessary for the framework to distinguish between the two **Create** actions. Without it, we would get an error message about an ambiguous action reference. Also, if there is only one action and it has an **HttpPost** filter, you will get a 404 error if you try to navigate to it with a GET.

> Filters are attributes that you can add to the controller or individual actions in the controller.
>
> Attributes are pieces of metadata that we can associate with pieces of code (classes, methods, properties, etc.). This metadata can be retrieved at run time through reflection and change the way the program behaves.
>
> The MVC framework uses filters and attributes a lot.

When added to the controller, filters affect every action in the class. When added to a specific method, only that action will be affected.

The **HttpPost** filter is part of a collection of attributes intended to influence when an action is available. These attributes include:

- AjaxOnly
- HttpDelete
- HttpGet
- HttpHead
- HttpPost
- HttpPut
- RequireHttps

AjaxOnly, **HttpGet**, and **HttpPost** will be the ones you will use most often. These filters come in handy for helping the framework tell the difference between actions with the same name since differences in the method signature can be difficult to determine because of the way the model binder works. There are also some nice security implications for these filters as well. It is a good practice to use **HttpPost** for data modifications such as creates, updates, and deletes. Posting data requires a form submission, so it prevents users from clicking a nefarious link in email messages and changing data by mistake.

Filters are not limited to method selection. We also have action filters such as:

- Timeout
- Cache
- Authorize
- HandleError

Filters provide an easy way to add security, limit access, or add performance enhancements such as caching and timeouts. There are also a couple of interfaces that you can implement to add your own arbitrary logic through filters.

Validations

Let's go back to our controller and set a breakpoint in the **Create** action to which we will post back. Run the app and click **Save**. When you hit the breakpoint, you will find that the data parameter has the data from the user when you click **Save**. This is because the model binder did its job. The model binder examined the forms collection, query string, cookies, etc., looking for IDs that matched the property names of the model. The model binder also handles type conversions and, as we will soon see, carries out input validations.

At this point, we have not explicitly stated any validation rules but the framework has inferred some basic rules based on data type. Because **When** is of type **DateTime**, any value that cannot be converted to a **DateTime** will fail validation. We get similar validations for **Duration**. Soon, we will add more validation rules.

Spend some time playing around with the **HttpPost Create** action. Enter values that are not valid for the data types in the model. For instance, enter "tomorrow" for **When** and "short" for **Duration**. When you click **Save**, the view returned will look like the following figure.

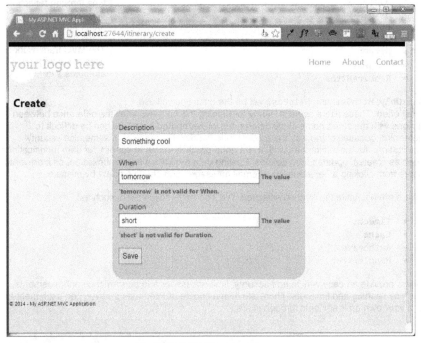

Figure 10: Validation messages

The messages come from the `ValidationMessageFor` calls that we added to the view in Code Listing 10. The text for the validation messages comes from the model binder, strictly based on the data types.

Additionally, if you check the breakpoint when you click **Save**, you will see that the properties without valid values will have null values. By poking around in the debugger, you may also notice that the model state complains about bad input.

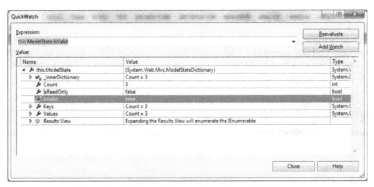

Figure 11: Quick watch showing invalid model state

This gives us a clue as to the next enhancement we will need to make to our action. We will need to make sure that the model state is valid before making any changes. Our updated action will now look like the following code listing.

```
[HttpPost]
public ActionResult Create(ItineraryItem data)
{
    if (ModelState.IsValid)
    {
        // Handle saving the data only if
        // the model state is valid
    }
    else
    {
        ModelState.AddModelError("",
            "The data you entered was not valid");
    }
    return View();
}
```

Code Listing 14: Action checking that the model is valid

In addition to checking the model state, we now add our own error message to the mix. The `AddModelError` method expects two parameters. The first one will specify where the message should be displayed and the second one will specify the message to be displayed. This first parameter should refer to the property from the model that caused problems, but because we are leaving it blank, our message will not be associated with any input control and will not be shown on the page until we modify the view to include a **ValidationSummary**. Add the following line to the top of the "**editor**" **div** tag in **Create.cshtml**.

```
@Html.ValidationSummary(true)
```

Code Listing 15: Adding a validation summary to the view

Passing **true** to the method will instruct the framework to not show error messages associated with properties. You will want this if you have validation messages associated with each property. With these changes in place, our view will look like the following figure after being submitted back to the controller.

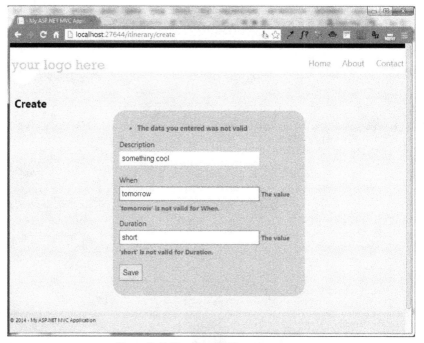

Figure 12: Editor with validation summary

Had we passed **false** to the **ValidationSummary**, then the property-specific messages would have appeared as well. In this case, they would be duplicated since they are also shown alongside each property's editor. We could leave off the individual calls to **ValidationMessageFor** and just rely on the summary to display all of the validation messages, but then we would lose context for the validation messages.

We will explore adding our own validations in greater detail in the next chapter.

Editors

Now, let's go back to the view and explore what else the framework can do for us to make the forms more intuitive. Consider this simple change:

```
@model MVCSuccinctly.Models.ItineraryItem
<h2>Create</h2>
<div class="editor">
@using (Html.BeginForm())
{
    @Html.ValidationSummary(true)
    <p>
        @Html.LabelFor(m => m.Description)
        @Html.EditorFor(m => m.Description)
        @Html.ValidationMessageFor(m => m.Description)
    </p>
    <p>
        @Html.LabelFor(m => m.When)
        @Html.EditorFor(m => m.When)

        @Html.ValidationMessageFor(m => m.When)
    </p>
    <p>
        @Html.LabelFor(m => m.Duration)
        @Html.EditorFor(m => m.Duration)
        @Html.ValidationMessageFor(m => m.Duration)
    </p>
    <p><input type="submit" value="Save"/></p>
}
</div>
```

Code Listing 16: Editor using EditorFor

We have replaced the calls to **TextBoxFor** with calls to **EditorFor**. When we run the app, we will see that it looks exactly the same.

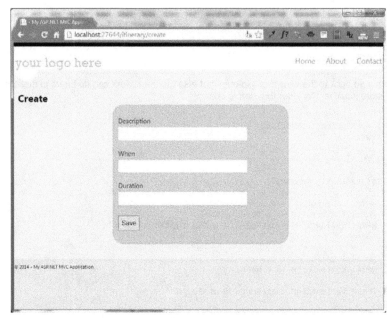

Figure 13: Output for EditorFor

So, what is the difference? In our original version, we explicitly state that we want a text box for the editor. In this second version, we allow the framework to determine which editor to use. As it turns out, the framework chose a text box as well, but that will not always be the case.

In fact, if you look closely, you will see a subtle difference in the Duration field when it has focus, as shown in the following figure.

Figure 14: Custom editor for integers

If you look at the generated markup, you will see that the text box used specifies one of the new HTML 5 types and, as long as the browser supports the **number** type, you will get a bit smarter text box. We get this new functionality because the Duration property is an integer.

```
<input class="text-box single-line" data-val="true"
    data-val-number="The field Duration must be a number."
    id="Duration" name="Duration" type="number" value="">
```

Code Listing 17: Input element with HTML 5 attributes

With this in mind, let's return to our model.

We will add a few new properties to showcase some built-in templates based on the type of the property. Let's add a Boolean and a nullable Boolean property.

```
public class ItineraryItem
{
    public DateTime? When { get; set; }
    public string Description { get; set; }
    public int? Duration { get; set; }
    public bool IsActive { get; set; }
    public bool? Confirmed { get; set; }
}
```

Code Listing 18: Extended itinerary item

The framework has its own logic for determining which editor to use, taking into account the data type and attributes associated with the property. This makes it easier to write our view. We do not have to worry about which editor to use; we can always use the more generic `EditorFor` and let the framework figure it out.

IsActive will need to have a value of true or false. **Confirmed** will also have a true or false value but could also not be set.

Now, if we add these new properties to the existing view in the same way as the previous properties (see Code Listing 15), we will get a view that looks like the following figure.

Figure 15: A Boolean and nullable Boolean editor in action

The framework knows that if the property is a Boolean, then there are only two values—a check box is the appropriate editor. But if the property can be null, then we have a third option—it switches to a drop-down menu with options for Not Set, True, and False. In our application, we did not have to do anything extra to get the drop-down menu.

Figure 16: Nullable Boolean options

Beyond the built-in templates that MVC already knows about, we can easily add our own templates.

Editors Based on Type

It would be nice to have a standard editor for dates. To make MVC treat properties of **DateTime** as it does Booleans, all we have to do is provide an editor template with the same name as the data type. To let MVC know about an editor template, simply place it in the folder **\Views\Shared\EditorTemplates**.

Our initial **DateTime.cshtml** should look like the following code sample.

```
@model DateTime?

@Html.TextBox("", (Model.HasValue ? Model.Value.ToShortDateString() :
string.Empty),
new { @class = "datePicker" , @readonly = "readonly"})
```

Code Listing 19: Custom Editor for DateTime

Once you get this basic editor working, play with it to make it your own. You may do this often. Being able to create your own editors is a substantial productivity boost. You can keep the markup simple as we have done so far, yet still have the resulting view be as sophisticated as you want.

This will create a text box. By leaving the first parameter blank, we allow the framework to fill it in and it will do so with the appropriate values to support data binding. The second parameter specifies the initial value for the text box. Here, we use the ternary operator to evaluate a conditional. If the value passed to it is set, we will display the result of calling **ToShortDateString** on the value. If the value is not set, we will display an empty string. We could just as easily display something such as "No Date Entered" or any other default value. The final parameter is an anonymous object whose properties will be treated as HTML attributes for the text box. In this case, we specify the CSS class and make it read-only.

I will often partner this with some JavaScript to add a jQueryUI date picker based on the class being **datePicker**. Dates are difficult to validate. Also, they are often difficult for a user to properly enter. To simplify this data entry and validation on the client side, it is a good idea to provide an editor that will help steer the user toward providing the right input.

```
$(".datePicker").datepicker(
{
    showOn: "button",
    gotoCurrent: true,
    showAnim: 'fold',
    buttonImage: "/Content/calendar.png",
    buttonImageOnly: true
})
```

Code Listing 20: jQuery code to activate the date picker

Our rendered view will now look like the following figure.

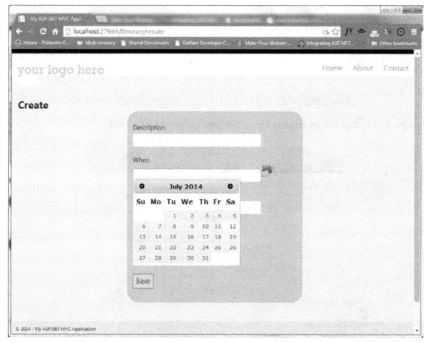

Figure 17: Custom editor for date picker

With this in place, any property of type **DateTime** will automatically get a nice date picker as its editor.

Editors Based on DataType

We are not limited to the data type to associate an appropriate editor. We can also use the **DataType** attribute on any property to specify an appropriate editor. This attribute, along with many others that we will be interested in, can be found in the **System.ComponentModel.DataAnnotations** namespace. This attribute allows us to draw distinctions within the same type in .NET.

For instance, we could redefine our **ItineraryItem** as in the following code listing.

```
public class ItineraryItem
{
    public DateTime? When { get; set; }
    [DataType(DataType.MultilineText)]
    public string Description { get; set; }
    public int? Duration { get; set; }
    public bool IsActive { get; set; }
    public bool? Confirmed { get; set; }
}
```

Code Listing 21: Forcing the Description to support multiple text lines

Now the Description will be rendered as a text area instead of a text box.

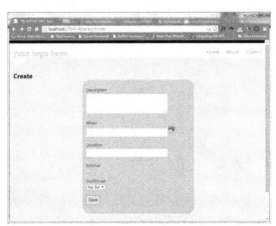

Figure 18: Text area as an Editor

The **DataTypeAttribute** provides several options to specify built-in templates that cannot be inferred from the data type. The **DataType** enumeration provides the following options:

- **CreditCard**: Represents a credit card number.
- **Currency**: Represents a currency value.
- **Custom**: Represents a custom data type.

- **Date**: Represents a date value.
- **DateTime**: Represents an instant in time, expressed as a date and time of day.
- **Duration**: Represents a continuous time during which an object exists.
- **EmailAddress**: Represents an email address.
- **Html**: Represents an HTML file.
- **ImageUrl**: Represents a URL to an image.
- **MultilineText**: Represents multiline text.
- **Password**: Represents a password value.
- **PhoneNumber**: Represents a phone number value.
- **PostalCode**: Represents a postal code.
- **Text**: Represents text that is displayed.
- **Time**: Represents a time value.
- **Upload**: Represents file upload data type.
- **Url**: Represents a URL value.

Most of these map directly to the new text types defined for HTML 5, so the default implementation will only work for browsers that support the new HTML 5 syntax.

Editors Based on UIHint

Finally, we have one more option for specifying an editor template; we can use something called a **UIHintAttribute**. Here, we explicitly give the name of a custom editor template to use. For example, we could define a custom editor template for phone numbers and associate it to a **ContactNumber** property as in the following code listing.

```
public class ItineraryItem
{
    public DateTime? When { get; set; }
    [DataType(DataType.MultilineText)]
    public string Description { get; set; }
    public int? Duration { get; set; }
    public bool IsActive { get; set; }
    public bool? Confirmed { get; set; }
    [UIHint("Phone")]
    public string ContactNumber { get; set; }
}
```

Code Listing 22: View model with a UIHint

Now, we can define an editor template, **Phone.cshtml**, and describe how the phone number should be edited.

```
@model string

@{
    var areaCode = string.Empty;
```

```
    var firstNumber = string.Empty;
    var secondNumber = string.Empty;
    if (Model != null)
    {
        areaCode = Model.Substring(0, 3);
        firstNumber = Model.Substring(3, 3);
        if (Model.Length >= 10)
        {
            secondNumber = Model.Substring(6, 4);
        }
    }
}
<input type="text" name="area_code" id="area_code"
    maxlength="3" size="3" value="@areaCode"/> -
<input type="text" name="number1" id="number1"
    maxlength="3" size="3" value="@firstNumber"/> -
<input type="text" name="number2" id="number2"
    maxlength="4" size="5" value="@secondNumber"/>
<input type="hidden" name="@ViewData.TemplateInfo.HtmlFieldPrefix"
    id="@ViewData.TemplateInfo.HtmlFieldPrefix"value="@Model"/>
<img src="../../../Content/images/Edit32.png" id="phoneNumberEdit"/>
<input type="text" name="unparsed" id="unparsed"/>
<script type="text/javascript">
    $(document).ready(function () {
        $("#unparsed").hide();
        var edit = $("#phoneNumberEdit");
        edit.click(function () { $("#unparsed").toggle(); });
        var phone = $('#area_code, #number1, #number2');
        phone.autotab_magic().autotab_filter('numeric');

        $("#unparsed").change(function () {
            var unparsed = $("#unparsed");
            var value = unparsed.val();

            value = value.replace(/\(|\)|\s|\-/gi, '');
            value = value.replace(/[a-zA-Z]+/gi, '');
            unparsed.val(value);
            $("#area_code").val(value.substring(0, 3));
            $("#number1").val(value.substring(3, 6));
            $("#number2").val(value.substring(6, 10));
            if (value.length == 10)
                unparsed.hide();
            var result = ($('#area_code').val()
                + $("#number1").val()
                + $("#number2").val());
            $("#@ViewData.TemplateInfo.HtmlFieldPrefix")
                .val(result);
        });
        phone.blur(function () {
            var result = ($('#area_code').val()
                + $("#number1").val()
                + $("#number2").val());
            $("#@ViewData.TemplateInfo.HtmlFieldPrefix")
```

```
                .val(result);
        });
    });
</script>
```

 Note: This example illustrates how these editor templates can become as complex as we need them to be. No matter how complex or simple the template is, we still access it by associating the appropriate attributes to the properties in the model, and always by using the `EditorFor` **HTML helper.**

Editors Based on Complex Types

Associating editor templates with data types is not limited to simple types. We can easily define new editor templates for any data type, including view models such as our **ItineraryItem**.

If we decided to move the markup for our current view into an editor template, our **ItineraryItem.cshtml** would look like the following code sample.

```
<p>
    @Html.LabelFor(m => m.Duration)
    @Html.EditorFor(m => m.Duration)
    @Html.ValidationMessageFor(m => m.Duration)
</p>
<p>
    @Html.LabelFor(m => m.IsActive)
    @Html.EditorFor(m => m.IsActive)
    @Html.ValidationMessageFor(m => m.IsActive)
</p>
. . .
<p>
    @Html.LabelFor(m => m.Confirmed)
    @Html.EditorFor(m => m.Confirmed)
    @Html.ValidationMessageFor(m => m.Confirmed)
</p>
```

Code Listing 24: Custom editor template

Our view can then be reduced to something as simple as this:

```
@model MVCSuccinctly.Models.ItineraryItem
<h2>Create</h2>
<div class="editor">
    @using (Html.BeginForm())
```

```
{
    @Html.ValidationSummary(true)
    @Html.EditorFor(m=>m)

    <p><input type="submit" value="Save"/></p>
}
</div>
```

Code Listing 25: Using the editor template

This is useful when a particular view model is a property of another view model, making interface composition easy for us.

Summary

We covered a lot of ground in this chapter and introduced several concepts that will be explored in greater detail later.

We have seen how the HtmlHelper functions work together to facilitate model binding. We saw our first filter used by the framework to mark an action as being accessible only as a POST or a GET.

We also went through a gentle introduction explaining how to show validation messages.

Finally, we delved into some subtle nuances for MVC's concept of editor templates. These templates are an exciting feature of MVC that make it easier to put together consistent input forms that are full of engaging functionality—without causing any headaches.

In the next chapter, we will take a closer look at the validation features made available in the framework.

Chapter 4 Don't Trust Everything the World Says

Validations are defined once as attributes on the properties of our models. With a bit of JavaScript, these validations will run in the user's browser. They will also run again back on the server as part of model binding. Running the validations in both locations may seem redundant, but in this day and age, validating the input supplied to a web app is not something that should be lightly undertaken. This approach is known as "defense in depth." For example, if a user skips our client-side validations and tries to directly post to the action, the server-side validations will still catch the bad input, preventing any harm from coming to our app.

 Tip: Client-side validations are really just a convenience for users who are playing by the rules; they should not be viewed as the only part of your app security.

 Note: Validations are important. Even more important is validating more than once. Even more important than validating more than once is not having to repeatedly define your validations. This sounds like a tall order, but the MVC framework covers us on all fronts.

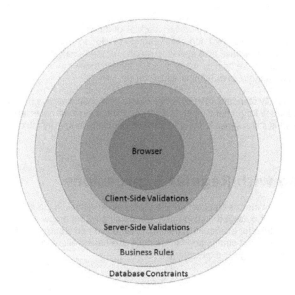

Figure 19: Defense in depth

Essential Validators

So, what do these validation attributes look like? It turns out they look similar to the attributes we have already used to select the editor templates. Let's go back to the **ItineraryItem** and add some appropriate validators.

```
public class ItineraryItem
{
    [Required (ErrorMessage =
        "You must specify when the event will occur")]
    public DateTime? When { get; set; }
    [Required(ErrorMessage =  "You must enter a description")]
    [MaxLength(140, ErrorMessage =
        "The description must be less than 140 characters.")]
    [DataType(DataType.MultilineText)]
    public string Description { get; set; }
    [Required (ErrorMessage =
        "You must specify how long the event will last")]
    [Range (1, 120, ErrorMessage =
        "Events should last between one minute and 2 hours")]
    public int? Duration { get; set; }
    public bool IsActive { get; set; }
    public bool? Confirmed { get; set; }
}
```

Code Listing 26: ItineraryItem view model with fundamental validation attributes

As you can see, we have added attributes to mark all of the properties as required. With this attribute added, the framework will add JavaScript client-side to ensure that the corresponding input field is not blank. We have also specified ranges for the **Duration** and set a **MaxLength** for the **Description**. All we have to worry about is adding these attributes. The framework will ensure that the appropriate JavaScript is added for us.

These are all generally standard validators to include. You should always have a smallest and a largest expected value for numeric input, even if you think a user will never exceed the range. Checking for them is still a sensible thing to do. You should also specify maximum lengths for string input.

Validating with Regular Expressions

Regular expression validators can play an important role in validating input. Explaining regular expressions in detail is outside the scope of this book as they are a powerful and complex technology. Fortunately, for examples in this book, we only need a subset of this power. We will only need to deal with short strings and fairly simple use cases, allowing us to avoid much of the complexity surrounding regular expressions.

Note: If you want to dig deeper and learn much more about regular expressions, Regular Expressions Succinctly is available as part of the Succinctly series.

```
public class ItineraryItem
{
    [Required (ErrorMessage =
        "You must specify when this event will occur")]
    public DateTime? When { get; set; }
    [Required(ErrorMessage = "You must enter a description")]
    [MaxLength(140, ErrorMessage =
        "The description must be less than 140 characters.")]
    [DataType(DataType.MultilineText)]
    public string Description { get; set; }
    [Required (ErrorMessage =
        "You must specify how long the event will last")]
    [Range (1, 120, ErrorMessage =
        "Events should last between one minute and 2 hours")]
    [RegularExpression (@"\d{1,3}", ErrorMessage =
        "Only numbers are allowed in the duration")]
    public int? Duration { get; set; }
    public bool IsActive { get; set; }
    public bool? Confirmed { get; set; }
}
```

Code Listing 27: ItineraryItem view model with regular expression attributes

Here, we have defined a regular expression for the **Duration** property, specifying that it must consist of one to three numbers. While this validation is not 100 percent accurate, it will suffice in conjunction with the other attributes. Our regular expression should limit the first digit to 1 and our other digits to 0, 1, or 2 if there are two or more digits in total. We should specify that the first digit cannot be 0, but in conjunction with the other validators, this will suffice.

We could also add a regular expression validator for the **When** property, but regular expressions are not well-suited for validating values such as dates.

Dates can quickly become tricky to deal with. The best way to handle dates on the client side is to use a good editor (as we saw in the last chapter) that creates well-formatted date strings, and then use the better facilities for parsing the string as a **Date** that are available on the server.

 Tip: Regular expressions are powerful but they are not always the right tool for the job. Used in the wrong places, they can cause many more problems than you are trying to solve. Always use them with care.

The following table provides a handy regular expression cheat sheet that should cover most of the scenarios you would need in your regular expression validators.

Table 1: Regular expression keywords

^	Matches the beginning of a string.
$	Matches the end of a string.
.	Matches any character except a new line.
*	Matches zero or more instances of the previous expression.
+	Matches one or more instances of the previous expression.
?	Matches zero or one instance of the previous expression.
{,}	Explicit range quantifier; specifies the min and max number of occurrences of the previous expression.
\w	Matches any word character.
\d	Matches any digit.
\s	Matches any white space.

The following table provides some regular expressions that might come in handy for validating input data in your MVC app.

Table 2: Common regular expressions

Social Security Number	`^\d{3}-\d{2}-\d{4}$`
Phone Number	`^(\(\d{3}\))|(\d{3}-?))\d{3}-?\d{4}$`
Zip Code	`^\d{5}(-\d{4})?$]`
Month Names	`^(Jan|Feb|Mar|Apr|May|Jun|Jul|Aug|Sep|Oct|Nov|Dec)$`
Password Complexity	`^(?=.*\d)(?=.*[a-z])(?=.*[A-Z]).{8,}$` // Just add whatever max length is appropriate

 Tip: As a rule of thumb, keep your regular expressions simple. Don't rely on them to cover all scenarios by themselves as they can, and likely will, quickly grow out of hand and become hard to manage.

Use regular expressions in conjunction with other validators to properly constrain your input. Many people will make the mistake of trying to use regular expressions to cover all of the cases they can see in their validation task. Always keep in mind that similar to all client-side validations, these are only meant to be a convenience to users who are playing by the rules. Multiple validators will, collectively, cover the various scenarios for user input.

Remote Validators

Sometimes you may have validation logic that cannot be easily expressed with the attributes we have seen so far. Sometimes we might even need access to real-time data from the database or some other source that is not easily accessible from the client side. Sometimes the validation logic is already implemented in business logic and we do not have any desire to implement it again on the client side.

To help with this task, we have remote validators. This simple attribute allows us to associate an action with the property, which the framework will then use to asynchronously call an external action or invoke business logic elsewhere in the app.

 Tip: Unlike the other attributes that we have seen so far in this chapter, this one is located in System.Web.MVC.

Following from previous examples, let's return to our **ItineraryItem** view model, and add a remote validator to ensure that the **When** property is not already overbooked.

```
public class ItineraryItem
{
    [Required (ErrorMessage =
        "You must specify when this event will occur")]
    [Remote("VerifyAvailability", "Itinerary")]
    public DateTime? When { get; set; }
    [Required(ErrorMessage =  "You must enter a description")]
    [MaxLength(140, ErrorMessage =
        "The description must be less than 140 characters.")]
    public string Description { get; set; }
    [Required (ErrorMessage =
        "You must specify how long the event will last")]
    [Range (1, 120, ErrorMessage =
        "Events should last between one minute and 2 hours")]
    [RegularExpression (@"\d{1,3}", ErrorMessage =
        "Only numbers are allowed in the duration")]
    public int? Duration { get; set; }
    public bool IsActive { get; set; }
    public bool? Confirmed { get; set; }
}
```

Code Listing 28: ItineraryItem with a remote validator

There are a couple of subtle points worth mentioning with this attribute. The first parameter is the name of the action. The second parameter is the name of the controller. When we specify the controller, remove the word **Controller** from the name. Even though the controller will generally be the same controller associated with the view, you still must explicitly specify it.

 Note: By convention, all controllers will have the word "Controller" in their name but it is left out of the name when building up a route or referring to a URL. For example, the Remote *attribute in* <u>Code Listing 28</u> *will properly refer to the* ItineraryController *as* Itinerary; *references to* ItinearyController *would result in routing errors.*

Now, let's look at the action in the controller.

```
[HttpGet()]
public JsonResult VerifyAvailability(DateTime When)
{
    return Json(true, JsonRequestBehavior.AllowGet);
}
```

Code Listing 29: Remote validation action

Here we have stripped out all of the business logic. You would retrieve the count of itinerary items for the logged-in user for this particular day and compare this against some configured threshold.

What you actually do in the action is entirely up to you.

Hard-coding a return value of **true** ensures that the method will pass all validations while returning false would fail all validations.

Sometimes we need more than one field to implement the remote validation. Perhaps we need both the **Description** and the **When** to handle the validation. We just need to make a couple of changes. The first change is to our model.

Nothing beyond defining the action configuring the attribute was requir to enable the asynchronous callb

Without this suppor we would have had add JavaScript to make a remote call track the return valu and hide or show th validation message based on the response.

```
public class ItineraryItem
{
    [Required (ErrorMessage =
        "You must specify when this event will occur")]
    [Remote("VerifyAvailability", "Itinerary",
            AdditionalFields = "Description")]
    public DateTime? When { get; set; }
    [Required(ErrorMessage =  "You must enter a description")]
    [MaxLength(140, ErrorMessage =
        "The description must be less than 140 characters.")]
```

```
public string Description { get; set; }
[Required (ErrorMessage =
    "You must specify how long the event will last")]
[Range (1, 120, ErrorMessage =
    "Events should last between one minute and 2 hours")]
[RegularExpression (@"\d{1,3}",
        ErrorMessage = "Only numbers are allowed in the duration")]
public int? Duration { get; set; }
public bool IsActive { get; set; }
public bool? Confirmed { get; set; }
}
```

Code Listing 30: Remote validator with additional fields

Next, we update the controller.

```
public JsonResult VerifyAvailability(DateTime When, string Description)
{
    return Json(true, JsonRequestBehavior.AllowGet);
}
```

Code Listing 31: Remote validation action with multiple parameters

 ***Tip:** Any number of parameters can be specified; you just need to make sure they match the list specified in the* AdditionalFields *property of the attribute.*

MetadataTypeAttribute

Having seen all of the attributes that can be added to the properties of a model, we can imagine that, after a while, definitions can get cluttered and become hard to read. All of the attributes can distract from any logic that you may have in your model. Worse still, these attributes are vulnerable to being unexpectedly changed if you are using any form of code generation such as Text Template Transformation Toolkit (T4). Often, we may not track enough metadata to generate all of the necessary attributes again, so it would be nice if we had a way to protect the attributes when we generate code.

This is where the **MetadataTypeAttribute** comes into play. This is a single attribute added to the class that tells the framework where to find the other attributes. If attributes are then added to this partnered metadata type, they will remain safe when the model is regenerated in any way.

By using a **MetadataTypeAttribute**, our model can be reduced to the following code.

```
[MetadataType (typeof (ItineraryItemAttributes))]
public class ItineraryItem
```

```
{
    public DateTime? When { get; set; }
    public string Description { get; set; }
    public int? Duration { get; set; }
    public bool IsActive { get; set; }
    public bool? Confirmed { get; set; }
}
```

Code Listing 32: Adding a MetadataType to the view model

And the partnered **MetadataType** will look like this:

```
public class ItineraryItemAttributes
{
    [Required(ErrorMessage =
        "You must specify when this event will occur")]
    [Remote("VerifyAvailability", "Itinerary",
            AdditionalFields = "Description")]
    public object When { get; set; }
    [Required(ErrorMessage = "You must enter a description")]
    [MaxLength(140,ErrorMessage =
        "The description must be less than 140 characters.")]
    public object Description { get; set; }
    [Required(ErrorMessage =
        "You must specify how long the event will last")]
    [Range(1, 120, ErrorMessage =
        "Events should last between one minute and 2 hours")]
    [RegularExpression(@"\d{1,3}",
    ErrorMessage = "Only numbers are allowed in the duration")]
    public object Duration { get; set; }
}
```

Code Listing 33: MetadataType with attributes set

The data type of the properties in the **MetadataType** is not important; all that matters is that the framework is able to match the name. Also, understand that the **MetadataType** does not need to include all of the properties; it only needs to include the properties that have attributes associated with them.

Finally, while properties can be in the model but not in the partnered **MetadataType**, any property mentioned in the **MetadataType** must be in the associated model.

 Tip: If you automatically generate your model, it's always a good practice to specify a MetadataType in the generated file and place any attributes that are not generated in this partnered type.

Summary

We have seen how validators can easily be added to the properties in our model. The most common validators include marking a property as required, setting a maximum length, and specifying an acceptable range of values. These are simple validations that should be specified for most properties.

More complex validations are possible with regular expressions, even though we will often only use a small subset of the full regular expression syntax. Even then, our regular expressions can be streamlined because they will rarely be used on their own, given that generally they would be used in conjunction with other validators to ensure clean input.

We have also seen that for the most complex validation requirements, we can easily add remote validation to instruct the framework to make an asynchronous callback to the server to handle the validations in our own custom, code-based logic.

Finally, we have seen how we can move all of these attributes to a separate class that uses a partnered `MetadataType`, allowing us to protect the attributes—something that's especially important if we are generating our classes by using automated code generation.

Chapter 5 MVC Meets jQuery

Modern web apps are expected to be fast, engaging, and interactive. This means that the old model of full postbacks to get data or process partial data are no longer enough. Part of the problem with full postbacks is that we send and receive more data than is necessary. This distracts users, puts more of a load on the network and servers, and slows everything down.

MVC, combined with jQuery, makes it easy to avoid these pitfalls. We can limit the initial download to only what is immediately required and then retrieve the rest as needed. We can also update smaller sets of data as needed, asynchronously, without having to send everything back every time or wait until the user has edited all of the data before processing any of the results. This makes the app more engaging and more responsive.

Out of the gate, the templates for both intranet apps and Internet apps come ready to incorporate jQuery. At most, you may want to update to a later version of jQuery. If you do upgrade and need to support older versions of Internet Explorer (IE), cap yourself at the latest 1.x version. Starting with 2.0, jQuery dropped support for IE prior to version 9. If you know that you will not support the older versions of IE, upgrade to the latest 2.x version. The files will be substantially smaller.

NuGet Package Manager

NuGet is designed to make it easier to manage external libraries such as jQuery, and has been available in Visual Studio since Visual Studio 2010. You can access it from the **Tools** menu in Visual Studio.

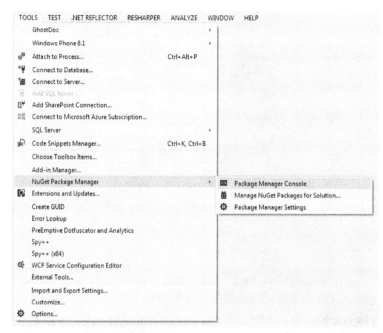

Figure 20: NuGet menu options

Select **Manage NuGet Packages for Solution** to get a list of the packages that have updates available.

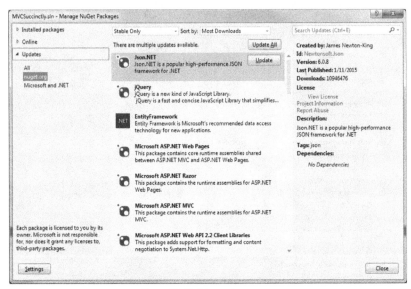

Figure 21: Update packages

You can easily update any package by simply clicking **Update**. This is convenient but can be problematic given the previous warnings about IE compatibility. The update command here will update you to the latest version, which may not be what you want.

 Tip: To update to a specific version, use the Package Manager Console *instead. From the console, enter the command:*

```
Install-Package jQuery -Version 1.11.2
```

If you press Tab after you type Version, you will get a list of the available versions. Simply select the version that you want.

JavaScript Background

Some basic familiarity with jQuery and JavaScript will be helpful at this point. It's highly advised that you have at least an idea of what jQuery is and how JavaScript works before proceeding with the rest of this chapter. In the sections that follow, we will focus on how jQuery interacts with MVC; this will not be a tutorial on how jQuery works.

Note: Syncfusion has many books in the Succinctly series, including titles on jQuery and JavaScript. Downloading them and keeping them handy as a reference for the rest of this chapter will help you a great deal.

Before we get started, let's review some best practices:

- AJAX endpoints should be actions in the controller responsible for the view. This keeps related functionality together. This action is free to do whatever it needs to do, but any developer should be able to go back to the controller to trace how the functionality is implemented.
- These actions should be configured to accept only POSTs. MVC will throw an exception when returning JSON from a GET, but this provides an extra layer of protection against leaking sensitive information.
- Actions should accept models as parameters where practical so the model binder will handle the conversions as well the validations.
- Actions should always strive to return `JsonResult` even if they are returning a single scalar type. This is the recommended transport type and jQuery will handle the conversions on the other end.

 Tip: Keep a good JavaScript reference handy.

With these best practices in mind, let's explore some possibilities. In the remaining part of this chapter, we will go through a couple of interactions that you are likely to see in a typical app:

- Download part of the page after the page has initially loaded.
- Retrieve text for help messages only if the user triggers the request.
- Delete an item from a list of items.

Download Part of the Page after the Page has Loaded

We may often find that part of the page may not be needed when the page first loads, but we do not necessarily want the user to have to do anything to get it. We do not want the user to miss it, but do not want to hold everything up waiting on the content.

For example, we might wait to download the menu until after the page has loaded. We might have advertising along the side that we want the user to see but not have to wait on. In both cases, we want to trigger an AJAX call at the appropriate point to ensure this happens as expected.

Note: Most calls of this nature are launched from the document ready event handler. This is a jQuery-provided piece of functionality that allows us to synchronize the loading of our MVC page with a piece of JavaScript so that the provided code will run once our MVC page is fully downloaded. You can find more about this event in any jQuery reference.

In this example, we will download some advertisements after the page has finished downloading. To do this, we need to add just a bit of markup in the page. We need to make sure that the page includes a **div** tag with an **id** of **ads**. We do not care where this tag is located or how it is styled. For our purposes, all we need is for the **id** to be properly set. Styling is entirely up to your app's style guides.

Our JavaScript code will look like the following code listing.

```
<script>
        $(document).ready(function() {
            $.ajax({
                url: '@Url.Action("GetAdsSimple")',
                dataType: "json",
                type: "POST",
                success: function(result) {
                    $("#ads").append(result);
                }
            });
        });
</script>
```

Code Listing 34: AJAX call to the GetAdsSimple action

As you can see, this will require an action in our controller called **GetAdsSimple**. We will call this method as a POST and expect JSON back. In this simple implementation, we will receive a raw string of formatted HTML.

 Note: Code Listing 34 includes a Razor call to the helper function Url.Action. This function is useful for creating the full URL. In this case, all we specified was the name of the action. This method will build out the rest to generate a complete URL, after making the assumption that the controller will be the same controller that served up the view.

A simple implementation could look like this:

```
[HttpPost]
public JsonResult GetAdsSimple()
{
    var data = new StringBuilder();
    data.Append("<ul>");
    data.Append("<li><img
        src='http://placehold.it/180x100'></li>");
```

```
    data.Append("<li><img
        src='http://placehold.it/180x100/ffffff/aaaaff'></li></ul>");
    return Json(data.ToString( ));
}
```

Code Listing 35: GetAdsSimple action

Here, we simply output a list of images. How you structure your markup is entirely up to you. If it is just a bit of markup, returning everything in a simple string may be all you need. But, if the markup is more complex or if you want the client to have more control over the generated HTML, we have other options.

 Note: Rarely will this be an acceptable option. A good best practice is to keep all markup out of the controller. This protects testability, plus we want to keep all of the look and feel considerations in the hands of the views.

Consider the following slightly more complex JavaScript code.

```
<script>
        $(document).ready(function() {
            $.ajax({
                url: '@Url.Action("GetAdParts")',
                dataType: "json",
                type: "POST",
                success: function(result) {
                    var content = "<ul>";
                    $.each(result, function (key, value) {
                        content += "<li ><a href = '"
                            + value.url + "' title='"
                            + value.caption + "'>"
                            + value.image + "</a></li>";
                    });
                    content += "</ul>";
                    $("#ads").append(content);
                }
            });
        });
</script>
```

Code Listing 36: AJAX call to GetAdParts

In this case, we have switched to calling a new action, **GetAdParts**, and this time, we expect the action to return a list of JSON objects that we will build up to produce the ads. This bit of extra complexity pulls generating the markup out of the controller and puts it back into the hands of the view. Different views could take these parts and format the ads differently based on whether they were being displayed on a desktop, tablet, or smartphone. You get a lot of power and flexibility by just transferring the ad parts and letting the client-side view decide how best to render these parts.

While the JavaScript might be a bit more complex, our action turns out to be a bit more straightforward because we can avoid all of the annoying string manipulation to generate the markup.

```
[HttpPost]
Public JsonResult GetAdParts()
{
    var data = new List<AdParts>();
    data.Add(new AdParts
    {
        image = "<img src='http://placehold.it/180x100'>",
        caption =
            "Lorem ipsum dolor sit amet, consectetur adipiscing elit".
        url = "http://#"
    });
    data.Add(new AdParts
    {
        image = "<img src='http://placehold.it/180x100'>", url = #",
        caption = "Donec adipiscing eros eget dui aliquet, nec tur."
    });
    return Json(data);
}
```

Code Listing 37: GetAdParts action

```
public class AdParts
{
    public string image { get; set; }
    public string url { get; set; }
    public string caption { get; set; }

}
```

Code Listing 38: AdParts definition

Either approach will give us a reasonably attractive set of ads as shown in the following figure.

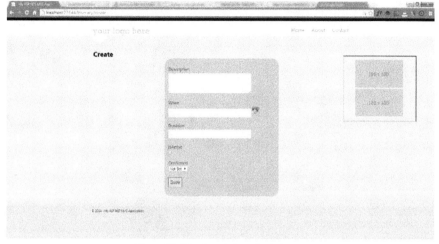

Figure 22: After the ads have loaded

Retrieve Help Text When the User Triggers the Request

This scenario is similar to the one we just created for showing advertisements; the main difference is that the AJAX call is now triggered by the user rather than automatically. Usually the user will click a trigger that will be used to initiate the action. In the following example, we will use an image that has a question mark to open the help and an X to close the help.

For this to work, we need two HTML components to be created. First, we need a **div** with an **id** of **helpTrigger**. Second, we need a **div** with an **id** of **helpContent**. How you set up these components depends on your style guidelines. Here, we will make the trigger a **div** tag that will be styled to pull its image from a sprite and a CSS that will ensure this image will always be in the upper right corner of the page. The CSS will look like the following code listing.

```
.helpTrigger {
    position: fixed;
    top: 1em;
    right: 1em;
    height: 50px;
    width: 50px;
    background: url('HelpClose.png') 0px 0px;
}

.closeTrigger {
    position: fixed;
    top: 1em;
```

```
    right: 1em;
    height: 50px;
    width: 50px;
    background: url('HelpClose.png') 0px 50px;
}

#helpContent {
    border: solid 1px black;
    border-right: 3em;
    min-height: 4em;
    border-radius: 1em;
    box-shadow: 1px 1px 15px black;
    position: fixed;
    top: 5em;
    right: 5em;
    height: 25em;
    width: 60em;
    overflow: auto;
    background-color: whitesmoke;
    padding: 1.5em;
}
```

Code Listing 39: Styling the helpTrigger and helpContent

Here, we have a sprite that includes two images that are each 50px by 50px.

Figure 23: A sprite for the help trigger and close trigger

For the help trigger, we want to display the top image and, to close it, we want to display the bottom image.

To add the trigger, we simply add our **div** tag anywhere we want to on the page.

```
<div id="helpTrigger" class="helpTrigger"></div>
```

Code Listing 40: The help trigger

To add the **helpContent**, we will add a similar **div** but note that we start with it hidden.

```
<div id="helpContent" style="display:none"></div>
```

Code Listing 41: Help content

Note: As a best practice, avoid using inline styles. This was done here merely to simplify the tutorial.

Once the **div** is in place, we will then use jQuery to add a different type of event handler called a **click** event. Similar to the **ready** event we used earlier in the chapter, this is functionality provided by jQuery, not by MVC. It allows us to be informed when the user clicks our **div** element. The event code will not only show our help text, it will also change the image sprite we placed in our **div** to convey the current opened or closed state of our text.

To simplify this switching around, we will define our event handlers as named functions in JavaScript instead of putting their implementations inline.

```javascript
function getHelp() {
    $.ajax({
        url: '@Url.Action("GetHelp")',
        dataType: "json",
        type: "POST",
        success: function (result) {
            $("#helpContent").empty().append(result);
            $("#helpContent").show();
            $("#helpTrigger").removeClass("helpTrigger")
                .addClass("closeTrigger");
            $("#helpTrigger").unbind("click");
            $("#helpTrigger").click(closeHelp);
        }
    });
}
```

Code Listing 42: AJAX call to GetHelp

```javascript
function closeHelp() {
    $("#helpContent").empty();
    $("#helpContent").hide();
    $("#helpTrigger").removeClass("closeTrigger")
        .addClass("helpTrigger");
    $("#helpTrigger").unbind("click");
    $("#helpTrigger").click(getHelp);
}
```

Code Listing 43: jQuery logic to close the helpContent

 Note: Here we rely on the action sending back formatted HTML, but all of the options that we explored in the previous example on how to structure and generate the markup are still available.

Our view, complete with the handy help trigger ready to bring us help, will look something like the following figure.

Figure 24: Our simple page showing the help trigger

And once the sprite image has been clicked, the help content, along with its close trigger, will look like the following.

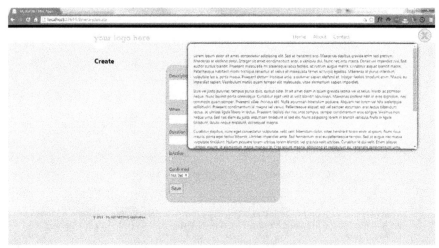

Figure 25: Our view showing the help content

Note: You would return something useful based on the originating page or some similar context. You may want to include maintenance of this help message in an admin section and simply retrieve formatted HTML from the database.

Delete an Item from a Grid

You may often display a list of items and allow users to click a trigger to remove an item from the list. This may be a list of messages to acknowledge, items in a shopping cart that can be removed, or a list of tasks that could be completed.

In each case, we need to call an action in the controller, passing the `id` for the item clicked. The controller will update the back end to remove the item from the list of items to display. When the AJAX call is finished, we will use jQuery to remove the item from the display.

Once again, we have a couple of special considerations regarding how we structure our markup.

Consider the following example list of itinerary items. We want users to be able to cancel any item as needed.

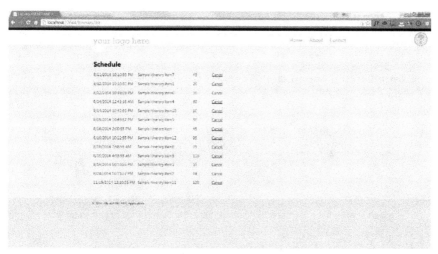

Figure 26: A grid with a cancel option for each item

```
<div id="Itinerary376">
    <div class="span10">8/11/2014 10:10:55 PM</div>
    <div class="span15">Sample itinerary item7</div>
    <div class="span5">45</div>
```

```
    <div class="span5 cancel"> Cancel</div>
</div>
<div id="Itinerary370">
    <div class="span10">8/12/2014 10:10:55 PM</div>
    <div class="span15">Sample itinerary item1</div>
    <div class="span5">20</div>
    <div class="span5 cancel"> Cancel</div>
</div>
<div id="Itinerary375">
    <div class="span10">8/12/2014 10:49:59 PM</div>
    <div class="span15">Sample itinerary item6</div>
    <div class="span5">30</div>
    <div class="span5 cancel"> Cancel</div>
</div>
    <div id="Itinerary373">
    <div class="span10">8/14/2014 12:41:18 AM</div>
    <div class="span15">Sample itinerary item4</div>
    <div class="span5">60</div>
    <div class="span5 cancel"> Cancel</div>
</div>
<div id="Itinerary379">
    <div class="span10">8/14/2014 10:43:55 PM</div>
    <div class="span15">Sample itinerary item10</div>
    <div class="span5">10</div>
    <div class="span5 cancel"> Cancel</div>
</div>
```

Code Listing 44: Markup to display a grid of itinerary items

If a user clicks the Cancel link (see the Tip that follows), we want to call an action in the controller. In this action, we should retrieve the item that the user selected and mark it as cancelled. Back in the web browser, we need to retrieve the parent of the cancel link and hide it.

 Tip: Even though I refer to this as a "Cancel link," it should be obvious from the markup that this is not a link; we just want it to look like one to the user. More importantly, we want to make sure that it does not look like one to a web crawler. It would truly be tragic for a web crawler to follow a bunch of links and cancel all of the events on your itinerary.

Any action that can manipulate data should be treated as a POST to prevent the user or a web crawler from accidentally "getting" data that could result in data manipulation.

```
.cancel {
    text-decoration: underline;
    cursor: pointer;
}
```

With this markup in place, we can add the event handlers as follows.

```
$(".cancel").click(function() {
    var id = ($(this).parent().attr("id"))
        .replace("Itinerary", "");
    var parent = $(this).parent();
        $.ajax({
            url: '@Url.Action("CancelItineraryItem")',
            dataType: "json",
            type: "POST",
            data : {id : id},
            success: function (result) {
                parent.hide();
            }
        });
    });
```

Code Listing 45: AJAX call to CancelItineraryItem action

 Note: The rules for this in JavaScript are subtle, but in this case, it refers to the element that triggered the event. We wrap it in a jQuery function call to convert it to a jQuery object. It is also worth noting that we have to put this in a local variable to be used by the success event handler because in this event handler, this will have a different meaning.

The fancy footwork with the parent, getting the **id**, and stripping off the key word **Itinerary** will give us the **id** that we will pass back to the action. This will be the unique identifier for the **ItineraryItem** back in the database.

Summary

In this chapter, we have seen how MVC can work with jQuery to create webpages that will load faster by reducing the amount of content that needs to be initially sent down. We explored two different options to trigger pulling down the rest of the content: automatically downloading the content after the page is fully loaded, and downloading the content when the user explicitly clicks a trigger. We have also seen how we can leverage jQuery to make AJAX calls to update part of the page, without having to refresh the entire page. Actions in controllers make natural endpoints for AJAX calls and the clean markup typical of MVC makes it easier to build effective selectors and control the markup through jQuery. jQuery and MVC combine well to facilitate creating dynamic, responsive web apps.

Chapter 6 MVC Scaffolding

In Chapter 2, while creating controllers and views, I noted that there were options to specify scaffolding templates. At the time, I suggested that you ignore these options, with the intention that we would return to them at a later point. In this chapter, we will explore those options in more detail.

It is helpful to understand how the pieces fit together before handing control over to something such as a scaffolder. Now that we have this background and perspective, let's explore what the framework and Visual Studio can do to simplify matters for us.

A scaffolder is a code generator designed to give you a head start on writing code. When you select a scaffolder, the code associated with that template will be evaluated to give you a starting point. In many cases, this takes care of a lot of the more tedious pieces of code. In some cases, the template may include comments offering guidance on what you need to do as you start working with the code.

Unlike most typical code generators, a scaffolder is not intended to be the end of the code. A scaffolder is not designed to provide the complete solution with all of the code that will be needed. Instead, a scaffolder allows you to start with the broad strokes laid out for you, with the expectation that you will fill in the rest. This is "one-time-only, code-only" code generation so you do not have to worry about losing any code changes that you make.

This is one of the most substantial productivity boosts that MVC offers.

Controllers

When you create a new controller, you can specify a template in the scaffolding options. So far, we have stayed with the default empty controller, but there are other built-in options available.

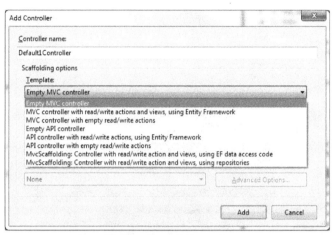

Figure 27: Controller scaffolding options

These templates provide varying degrees of boilerplate code that is already written for you. This is "one-time-only" code generation to jump-start your development. If, for example, you choose **MvcScaffolding: Controller with read/write action and views, using repositories**, you will have a fully functional controller with a complete set of views built with a set of well-architected classes for data access—all without writing any code yourself.

Depending on your development standards, this may be all that you need. Just specify the model and a repository, and let Visual Studio do the rest.

Thanks to the scaffolding, you do not have to look at an empty class and wonder what's next. Let the framework do as much of the heavy lifting as possible; you have enough to worry about.

Views

The scaffolding templates for views are much more modest. Specify a model and then select from one of six actions.

Figure 28: View scaffolding options

Table 3: Scaffolding template options

Create	Creates a view for creating a new instance of the associated model.
Delete	Creates a view that will display the details for the associated model along with prompts to delete the item.
Details	Creates a view for displaying a read-only copy of the associated model.
Edit	Creates a view for editing the details for an existing instance of the associated model.
Empty	Creates an empty view with no details from the associated model.
List	Creates a view that includes a table for showing the details for a list of model items.

You will get some decent markup.

```
<h2>Create</h2>

@using (Html.BeginForm())
{
    @Html.AntiForgeryToken()
    @Html.ValidationSummary(true)

    <fieldset>
        <legend>ItineraryItem</legend>

        <div class="editor-label">
            @Html.LabelFor(model => model.When)
        </div>
        <div class="editor-field">
            @Html.EditorFor(model => model.When)
            @Html.ValidationMessageFor(model => model.When)
        </div>

        <div class="editor-label">
            @Html.LabelFor(model => model.Description)
        </div>
        <div class="editor-field">
            @Html.EditorFor(model => model.Description)
            @Html.ValidationMessageFor(model => model.Description)
        </div>

        <div class="editor-label">
            @Html.LabelFor(model => model.Duration)
        </div>
        <div class="editor-field">
            @Html.EditorFor(model => model.Duration)
            @Html.ValidationMessageFor(model => model.Duration)
        </div>

        <div class="editor-label">
            @Html.LabelFor(model => model.IsActive)
        </div>
        <div class="editor-field">
            @Html.EditorFor(model => model.IsActive)
            @Html.ValidationMessageFor(model => model.IsActive)
        </div>

        <div class="editor-label">
            @Html.LabelFor(model => model.Confirmed)
        </div>
        <div class="editor-field">
            @Html.EditorFor(model => model.Confirmed)
            @Html.ValidationMessageFor(model => model.Confirmed)
        </div>

        <div class="editor-label">
            @Html.LabelFor(model => model.ContactNumber)
        </div>
```

```
<div class="editor-field">
    @Html.EditorFor(model => model.ContactNumber)
    @Html.ValidationMessageFor(model => model.ContactNumber)
</div>

<p>
    <input type="submit" value="Create"/>
</p>
</fieldset>
}

<div>
    @Html.ActionLink("Back to List", "Index")
</div>

@section Scripts {
    @Scripts.Render("~/bundles/jqueryval")
}
```

Code Listing 46: Generated editor

In most cases, you should be able to get the look you want without changing anything in the generated markup beyond reordering the controls. Remember from our earlier discussions that the `EditorFor` HTML helper can be quite sophisticated in finding the correct editor.

Whether the views are created by the controller scaffolding or the views scaffolding, you will get the same markup. But what if you do not like this markup or the code generated for the controller? Are there any other options?

Enter Text Template Transformation Toolkit

The code generated by the scaffolding templates uses the Text Template Transformation Toolkit, or T4. T4 is one of the best-kept secrets in .NET development.

This is a toolkit for creating code generators regardless of the language of the code being generated. In fact, calling it a code generator sells it short. We can use T4 to generate any text-based output. T4 transforms metadata through the template we specify to generate an appropriate output. This metadata can be input from any of the following scenarios:

- C# code
- VB.NET code
- SQL code
- HTML
- Razor
- Change logs

We can drive the code generation with any .NET language, typically C# or VB.NET. Our examples will all use C#.

Because the scaffolding templates are based on T4, we can edit these templates to change the code that is generated. You may want to do this to create a controller template that is based on NHibernate instead of Entity Framework, or you may want to create a list view template that does not use a table to display the list. The possibilities are limited only by your imagination.

A full discussion of T4 is beyond the scope of this book, but we will not need all of the capabilities of T4 here. In general, our changes will be minor.

First, we need to find the templates used by the scaffolding so that we can edit them to do what we require. These templates are stored with your installation of Visual Studio. So, the full path depends on whether you are running 32-bit or 64-bit, your version of Visual Studio, the language you want to end up with, and which view engine you are using. To find the templates used by a 32-bit version of Visual Studio 2013 for C# using Razor, look in:

C:\Program Files (x86)\Microsoft Visual Studio 12.0\Common7\IDE\ItemTemplates\CSharp\Web\MVC 4\CodeTemplates\AddView\CSHTML

And

C:\Program Files (x86)\Microsoft Visual Studio 12.0\Common7\IDE\ItemTemplates\CSharp\Web\MVC 4\CodeTemplates\AddController

Figure 29: View template location

Figure 30: Controller template location

Let's start by looking at **Empty.tt**. This will be the simplest template because it literally creates an empty shell with no regard for the metadata associated with the model.

By default, when you open a .tt file in Visual Studio, it will look a bit rough with no syntax highlighting. This is true through community previews for Visual Studio 2015.

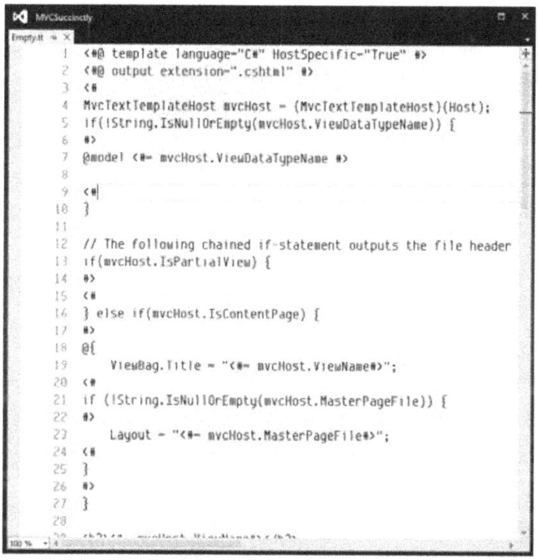

Figure 31: Editing a template without an extension

Syntax highlighting is always nice but it is even more important for a code generator—especially if the language used to drive the generation is the same language that will be generated. If you are using C# to generate C#, it can be difficult to separate template code from generated code.

We are also missing IntelliSense support out of the box. This is, potentially, a huge hurdle. IntelliSense is a substantial productivity boost. We all feel the impact if it is missing. Finally, out of the box, there is no support for debugging the template. This will probably not be a big deal initially, but eventually your templates may become complex enough that you will need this type feature.

Fortunately, there are several extensions available to fill in this gap.

The screenshots and discussions that follow are based on the Tangible T4 extension.

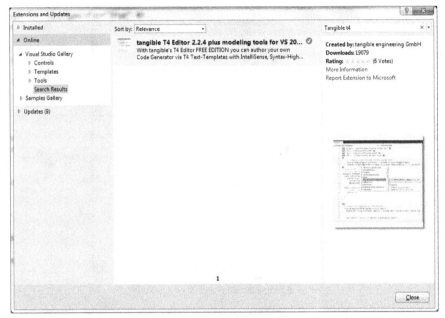

Figure 32: The Tangible T4 extension

This will add some much needed syntax highlighting and IntelliSense support.

 Note: The Tangible extension is the one that I use. There are others available, so it's worth looking around. Tangible is available as a free community version and a paid professional version. If you plan on doing anything major with T4, the professional version is worth the investment.

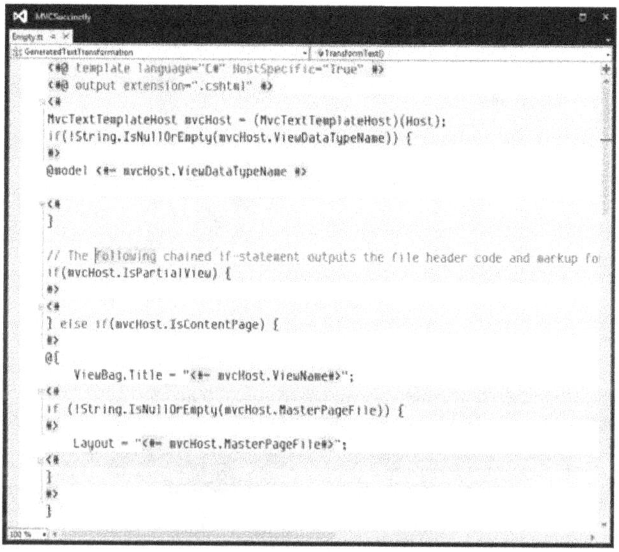

Figure 33: Editing with an extension

With syntax highlighting, the structure of the file becomes easier to navigate and understand.

The first two lines are T4 directives stipulating the language and file extension for the generated file. If you've ever used ASPX files in any of your previous projects, there's a good chance that the T4 syntax will immediately make sense to you. The basic tags are as follows:

- `<#=   #>` specifies variable substitution.
- `<#     #>` delimits a code block.
- `<#@ assembly name = ""  #>` defines a referenced assembly used by your T4 code.
- `<#@ import namespace = ""  #>` defines a referenced namespace that will be used by your T4 code.

The Tangible editor also gives us a new menu with an option to **Collapse all T4**.

TANGIBLE T4   TOOLS   TEST   ARC

🔍 Template Gallery
▶ Debug Template
🔧 Debug in new VS
⟟ Collapse all T4
⟟ Expand all T4
◎ Help
ⓘ Support
✕ Options
⊟ Activate Pro Features

Figure 34: Tangible T4 menu

This will collapse all of the T4 code blocks and leave us with just the generated code. This makes it a lot easier to see what the output will look like.

```
<#@ template language="C#" HostSpecific="True" #>
<#@ output extension=".cshtml" #>
⊞<#...#>
@model <#= mvcHost.ViewDataTypeName #>

⊞<#...#>
⊞<#...#>
@{
    ViewBag.Title = "<#= mvcHost.ViewName#>";
⊞<#...#>
    Layout = "<#= mvcHost.MasterPageFile#>";
⊞<#...#>
}

<h2><#= mvcHost.ViewName#></h2>
⊞<#...#>
@{
    Layout = null;
}

<!DOCTYPE html>

<html>
<head>
    <meta name="viewport" content="width=device-width" />
    <title><#= mvcHost.ViewName #></title>
</head>
<body>
⊞<#...#>
```

Figure 35: Empty.tt with T4 code collapsed

Study the way the generated code looks in the template. Compare this to the code that is generated. At this point, we do not really care about the T4 code used to drive the generation. We are more interested in the final product.

Edit.tt

Let's move on to the **Edit.tt** file. This template is much more interesting because it loops through the properties in the specified model. The easiest change to make is to add comments to the generated output. Let's start by simply adding a comment to give the developer a bit of guidance about what needs to be done next.

Our template should now look like the following figure.

Figure 36: Our updated editor template

Once we have created a new `Edit` view, we can see the results of this simple change.

```
@model MVCSuccinctly.Models.ItineraryItem

@{
```

```
    ViewBag.Title = "Edit";
}
<!-- provides an Editor for each property in MVCSuccinctly.Models.ItineraryItem --
>
<h2>Create3</h2>

@using (Html.BeginForm()) {
    @Html.AntiForgeryToken()
    @Html.ValidationSummary(true)

    <fieldset>
        <legend>ItineraryItem</legend>

        @Html.HiddenFor(model => model.Id)

        <div class="editor-label">
            @Html.LabelFor(model => model.When)
        </div>
        <div class="editor-field">
            @Html.EditorFor(model => model.When)
            @Html.ValidationMessageFor(model => model.When)
        </div>
```

Code Listing 47: Generated code with our new comment

Now let's move on to something a bit more interesting. Suppose your style wants to group a label, input control combination as a unit, and be able to show two per line. To support this, let's wrap the two in a **div** tag.

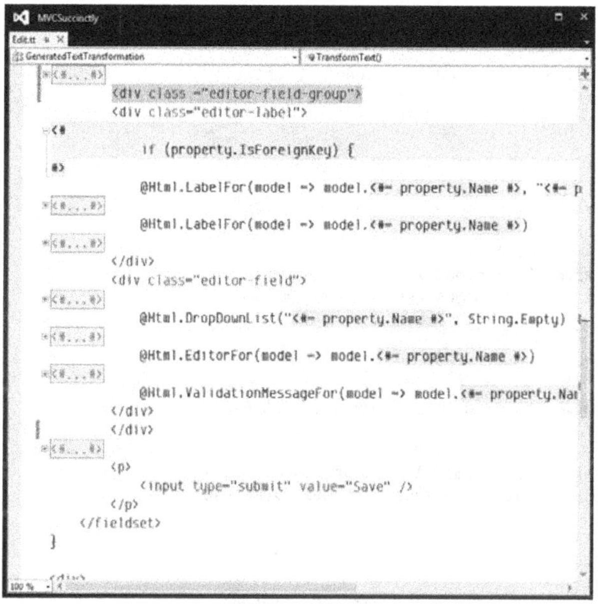

Figure 37: Our editor, updated to support a two-column layout

Here, we have added a new **div** tag that wraps around both the label and the input control. Now when we create a new view, we get the following:

```
@using (Html.BeginForm()) {
@Html.AntiForgeryToken()
@Html.ValidationSummary(true)

<fieldset>
<legend>ItineraryItem</legend>

    @Html.HiddenFor(model => model.Id)

    <div class="editor-field-group">
        <div class="editor-label">
            @Html.LabelFor(model => model.When)
        </div>
        <div class="editor-field">
            @Html.EditorFor(model => model.When)
            @Html.ValidationMessageFor(model => model.When)
        </div>
    </div>
    <div class="editor-field-group">
        <div class="editor-label">
            @Html.LabelFor(model => model.Description)
```

```
        </div>
        <div class="editor-field">
            @Html.EditorFor(model => model.Description)
            @Html.ValidationMessageFor(model => model.Description)
        </div>
    </div>
    <div class="editor-field-group">
        <div class="editor-label">
            @Html.LabelFor(model => model.Duration)
        </div>
        <div class="editor-field">
            @Html.EditorFor(model => model.Duration)
            @Html.ValidationMessageFor(model => model.Duration)
        </div>
    </div>
    <div class="editor-field-group">
        <div class="editor-label">
            @Html.LabelFor(model => model.IsActive)
        </div>
        <div class="editor-field">
            @Html.EditorFor(model => model.IsActive)
            @Html.ValidationMessageFor(model => model.IsActive)
        </div>
    </div>
    <div class="editor-field-group">
        <div class="editor-label">
            @Html.LabelFor(model => model.Confirmed)
        </div>
        <div class="editor-field">
            @Html.EditorFor(model => model.Confirmed)
            @Html.ValidationMessageFor(model => model.Confirmed)
        </div>
    </div>
    <div class="editor-field-group">
        <div class="editor-label">
            @Html.LabelFor(model => model.ContactNumber)
        </div>
        <div class="editor-field">
            @Html.EditorFor(model => model.ContactNumber)
            @Html.ValidationMessageFor(model => model.ContactNumber)
        </div>
    </div>
    <p>
        <input type="submit" value="Save"/>
    </p>
</fieldset>
```

Code Listing 48: Generator output supporting two columns

I've noted my changes in Code Listing 48 in bold to make it easier to see what I've changed from the original file.

Adding Our Own T4 Code

Continuing with the example that we have been building upon, let's create a completely custom file. Let's modify the generated markup to draw a distinction between the columns in our two-column display. We will keep track of whether or not the input control is in the first column or the second column.

This contrived example will allow us to define some conditional logic where we determine whether or not this is an even or an odd input control set.

To support this, we will add two new style sheet classes—**even** and **odd**—that will be added to the `editor-field-group` tag.

To determine which class to add to each of our `editor-field-group`s, we need to keep track of how many input controls we have added so far. If this count is even, then we will add the class **even**. If it is odd, then we will add the class **odd**. Our updated template should now look like the following.

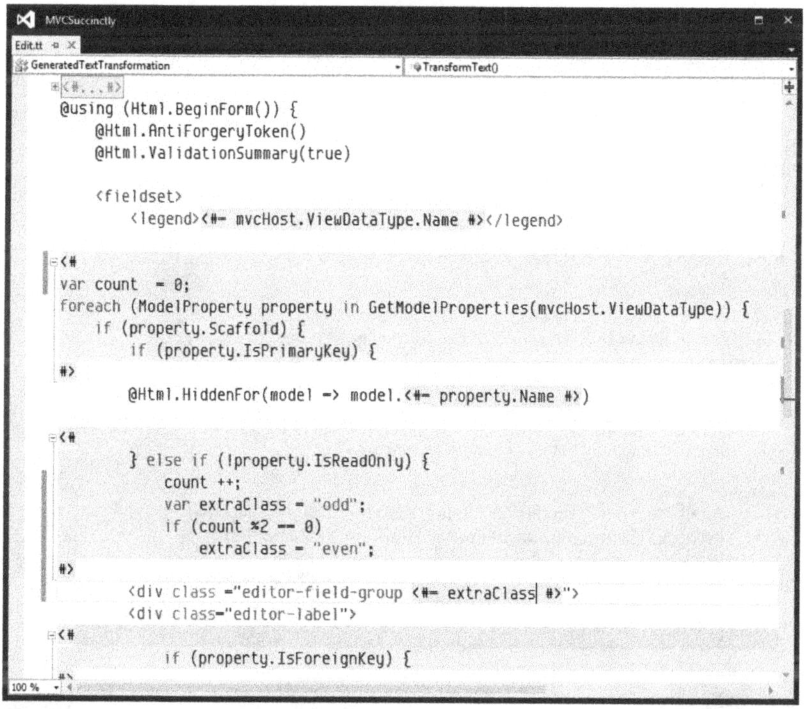

Figure 38: Updated template without our logic added

Note: There are many ways of using T4 technology to help provide solutions to the scenarios highlighted in this section. The path I've chosen here is just one of those ways. I encourage you to experiment and develop others to meet any of your needs and to fulfill any requirements your projects may have.

The generated code will look like the following code listing.

```
@using (Html.BeginForm()) {
@Html.AntiForgeryToken()
@Html.ValidationSummary(true)

<fieldset>
    <legend>ItineraryItem</legend>

    @Html.HiddenFor(model => model.Id)

    <div class="editor-field-group odd">
        <div class="editor-label">
            @Html.LabelFor(model => model.When)
        </div>
        <div class="editor-field">
            @Html.EditorFor(model => model.When)
            @Html.ValidationMessageFor(model => model.When)
        </div>
    </div>
    <div class="editor-field-group even">
        <div class="editor-label">
            @Html.LabelFor(model => model.Description)
        </div>
        <div class="editor-field">
            @Html.EditorFor(model => model.Description)
            @Html.ValidationMessageFor(model => model.Description)
        </div>
    </div>
    <div class="editor-field-group odd">
        <div class="editor-label">
            @Html.LabelFor(model => model.Duration)
        </div>
        <div class="editor-field">
            @Html.EditorFor(model => model.Duration)
            @Html.ValidationMessageFor(model => model.Duration)
        </div>
    </div>
    <div class="editor-field-group even">
        <div class="editor-label">
            @Html.LabelFor(model => model.IsActive)
        </div>
        <div class="editor-field">
            @Html.EditorFor(model => model.IsActive)
            @Html.ValidationMessageFor(model => model.IsActive)
        </div>
    </div>
```

```
    </div>
    <div class="editor-field-group odd">
        <div class="editor-label">
            @Html.LabelFor(model => model.Confirmed)
        </div>
        <div class="editor-field">
            @Html.EditorFor(model => model.Confirmed)
            @Html.ValidationMessageFor(model => model.Confirmed)
        </div>
    </div>
    <div class="editor-field-group even">
        <div class="editor-label">
            @Html.LabelFor(model => model.ContactNumber)
        </div>
        <div class="editor-field">
            @Html.EditorFor(model S=> model.ContactNumber)
            @Html.ValidationMessageFor(model => model.ContactNumber)
        </div>
    </div>
    <p>
        <input type="submit" value="Save"/>
    </p>
</fieldset>
}
```

Code Listing 49: Output from the generated code updated to support even and odd columns

With a bit of creativity and patience, T4 opens up a lot of possibilities. We have stepped through a couple of contrived examples here, but there is a great deal of power at your disposal.

Summary

In this chapter, we have seen how Visual Studio can write much of the code for controllers and views. Scaffolding includes built-in templates that can automatically add most of the code needed to have a fully functional controller with associated views to support basic create, read, update, and delete operations.

We have also seen how we can extend the built-in templates by changing the associated T4 templates. Changes can be simply including comments in the generated code, or complex additions to the T4 code.

Road Map for Further Reading

I have kept this book brief by staying tightly focused on models, views, and controllers. We have left out a lot of ancillary topics, but modern web apps are not so isolated. They exist in a wider context of browser compatibility, web standards, data access, aesthetic designs, and subtle nuances of business logic.

Fortunately, Syncfusion has a growing library of *Succinctly* books ready to fill in these gaps and enable you to fully explore the topics that come into play in the wider context of building a modern web app.

With that in mind, here is a convenient road map for continued reading through the *Succinctly* series:

ASP.NET MVC 4 Mobile Websites Succinctly	Discusses using the MVC framework to build websites optimized for mobile devices.
Twitter Bootstrap 3 Succinctly	Twitter Bootstrap is a CSS library for building visually engaging websites. This library gives you a great starting point to having consistent typography, a responsive grid, consistent font-based icons, and cross-browser support. This book gives you all of the details needed to effectively use this library.
JavaScript Succinctly	Anything you want to do client-side will involve JavaScript. Regardless of what library or framework you may use on top of JavaScript, a good foundation in the fundamentals of JavaScript will serve you well. This book gives you the foundational material that you will need to effectively use JavaScript.
jQuery Succinctly	jQuery is a common and essential library built on top of JavaScript to help your web apps come alive. jQuery shields you from most of the browser inconsistencies in implementing JavaScript, allowing you to focus more on business logic and user experience and less on arcane JavaScript implementation details.
Knockout.js Succinctly	Knockout.js is a JavaScript library that brings the concepts of Model View ViewModel (MVVM) to client-side programming. This library includes declarative bindings, templating, UI updates, and more. This book gives you the knowledge to effectively use this library to create immersive web apps

without getting bogged down in JavaScript details when keeping the UI updated with changes to the underlying data model.

AngularJS Succinctly	AngularJS is a JavaScript library that brings MVVM to the client side. AngularJS is different from Knockout in a couple of key ways. AngularJS adapts and extends traditional HTML to make it behave more like it was designed to, with dynamic web apps in mind.
Regular Expressions Succinctly	We touched on regular expressions briefly in Chapter 4 when we discussed validations, but we only scratched the surface. This book is a handy reference for taking your regular expression validations to the next level.
NHibernate Succinctly	Every web app will eventually persist data in a database. NHibernate is one approach that allows you to deal with data access logic in terms of objects instead of writing all of your SQL by hand. This comprehensive guide gives you everything you need, from installation to profiling.
Entity Framework Code First Succinctly	Entity Framework is Microsoft's solution for data access. This book guides you through the methodology of starting with your code and allowing Entity Framework to infer everything needed to generate a database for you. This book covers everything from design best practices, to profiling and optimization to avoid common pitfalls.
Windows Azure Web Sites Succinctly	Cloud computing is the buzzword of the day, and Azure is Microsoft's cloud solution. This books gives you all of the details needed to understand where and how your web apps can fit into this cloud platform.

www.ingramcontent.com/pod-product-compliance
Lightning Source LLC
Chambersburg PA
CBHW071305050326
40690CB00011B/2532